PATRICK MAHOMES

THE BOY WHO BECAME A STAR QUARTERBACK

This book belongs to

_____

CONTENTS

CHAPTER 1

Early Years

Once upon a time in Tyler, Texas, there was a spirited and energetic little boy named Patrick Mahomes. Even from a young age, Patrick was bursting with curiosity and a love for life. His laughter echoed through the halls of his family home, bringing joy to everyone around him.

Patrick came from a close-knit family that believed in the power of love and support. His parents, Pat and Randi Mahomes, were not just mom and dad; they were his biggest cheerleaders. As the son of a former professional baseball player, Pat Mahomes Sr., Patrick grew up surrounded by the excitement of sports.

In those early days, the Mahomes household was filled with the sounds of cheering for their favorite teams. Little Patrick would sit wide-eyed, watching games with his family, soaking in the thrill of competition. It was during these moments that the seeds of his love for sports were planted.

From a tiny tot, Patrick showed a keen interest in anything that involved a ball. Whether it was tossing a football with his dad in the backyard or shooting hoops with his friends, he was drawn to the world of athletics. His family noticed his passion and encouraged him to explore different sports, letting him discover where his heart truly belonged.

As Patrick grew, so did his enthusiasm for sports. His family stood by him, nurturing his love for the game and instilling in him the values of hard work and dedication. Little did they know, this energetic kid would one day become a shining star on the football field, inspiring children everywhere to dream big.

And so, the journey of Patrick Mahomes began, with the echoes of laughter and the love of a family that set the stage for the incredible adventures that awaited him.

CHAPTER 2

High School Phenomenon

As Patrick Mahomes entered his teenage years, he went to Whitehouse High School in Whitehouse, Texas. He didn't just stick to one sport; he embraced the thrill of football, baseball, and basketball. Whether tossing a football with friends, hitting home runs on the baseball diamond, or shooting hoops on the basketball court, Patrick's days were filled with the joy of play.

He believed that each sport contributed to his skills on the football field. Playing basketball improved his agility, and pitching in baseball honed his quarterback skills.

In his senior year of high school, Patrick's performances were spectacular. He threw the football for an incredible 4,619 yards, scored 50 touchdowns with his throws, ran for 948 yards, and scored 15 rushing touchdowns. The cheers of his fans echoed through the stadium as Patrick showcased his extraordinary talents.

But it wasn't just football where Patrick excelled. On the baseball field, he achieved something truly special – a no-hitter with an impressive 16 strikeouts in a single game. For his remarkable achievements in high school sports, he was honored as the Maxpreps Male Athlete of the Year for 2013–2014.

Even as a high school student, Patrick was a sought-after talent. Rivals.com rated him as a three-star football recruit and the 12th best dual-threat quarterback in his class. Offers came in from Texas Tech, Rice, and Houston, but Patrick decided to commit to Texas Tech University, following his passion for football.

Interestingly, Patrick was also a top prospect for the 2014 Major League Baseball draft. The Detroit Tigers even selected him in the 37th round, but Patrick chose not to sign a contract because he was committed to his love for football and Texas Tech.

And so, in the small town of Whitehouse, the journey of Patrick Mahomes from a multi-sport enthusiast to a football sensation began, paving the way for the remarkable chapters that lay ahead.

CHAPTER 3

College Years

In his first year at Texas Tech, Patrick Mahomes came onto the football field eager to learn and play. At the start, Mahomes served as a backup to Davis Webb. During a game against Oklahoma State, when Webb got injured, Patrick took the field for the first time. In that game, he completed two passes for 20 yards, throwing a spectacular touchdown but also facing a little hiccup with an interception.

As destiny would have it, Mahomes got the chance to start his first career game against the Longhorns team. The young quarterback completed 13 passes for 109 yards, showing the world that a new star was rising. He continued as the starting quarterback for the last three games of the season, leaving a trail of awe-inspiring moments.

As Patrick entered his sophomore year, he took on the role of starting quarterback for Texas Tech. With determination and skill, he led the Red Raiders to a 7–6 season, creating magic on the football field.

Throughout the season, Patrick's arm dazzled, with ten games going over 350 passing yards and four games surpassing 400. His incredible performance included a five-touchdown game against Iowa State. By the end of the season, he led the Big 12 Conference with impressive stats: 4,653 passing yards, 36 touchdowns, and 15 interceptions.

Even as he shone on the football field, Patrick didn't forget his love for baseball. He played in three games, showcasing his talent as a pitcher.

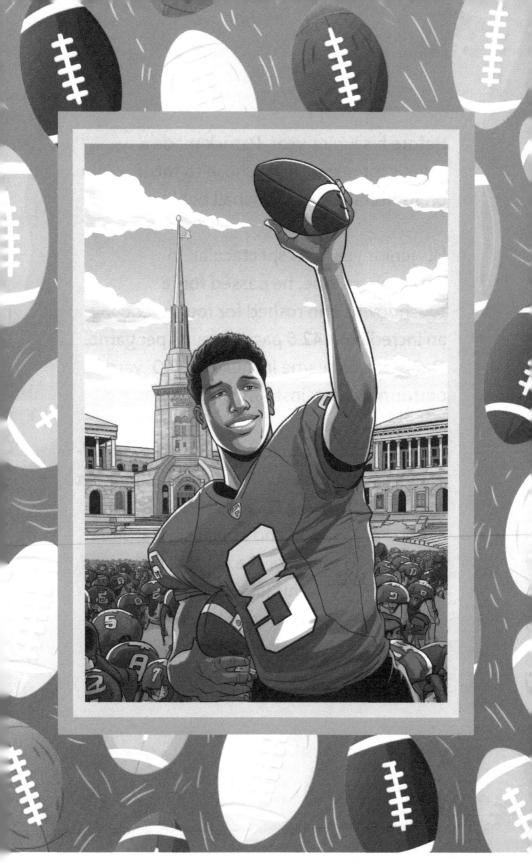

Before his junior year, Patrick made a significant decision: he chose to focus solely on football, leaving baseball behind.

His junior year was spectacular. In September alone, he passed for 18 touchdowns and rushed for four, averaging an incredible 442.5 passing yards per game. One standout game included a 540-yard performance against Arizona State.

The highlight of the season came in a record-breaking game against Oklahoma. Patrick set multiple NCAA, Big 12, and school records, earning admiration and applause. Despite the ups and downs of the season, Mahomes finished strong in his final game with Texas Tech, securing a victory with 586 passing yards and six touchdowns against Baylor.

By the end of his junior year, Patrick Mahomes had not only led the country in various statistics but had also been honored with the Sammy Baugh Trophy for being the nation's top college passer. He was also recognized with an Academic All-America second team award, showcasing his remarkable achievements in college sports.

On January 3, 2017, Patrick made a big announcement – he would forgo his last year of college eligibility and enter the NFL Draft, ready to take on new challenges and make his mark at the professional level. The next adventure awaited the young quarterback as he set his sights on the NFL.

CHAPTER 4

Draft Day and Rookie Season

Before Patrick Mahomes became an NFL superstar, there were days filled with excitement and anticipation. Scouts and analysts predicted that he would be chosen in the first or second round of the NFL draft to showcase his incredible skills that had dazzled fans during his college days.

During a special event called the NFL Scouting Combine, where future NFL players showcase their talents, Patrick stood out. In the throwing drills, his passes were like lightning, clocked at an amazing 60 mph, tying the record for the fastest pass ever recorded at the Combine. Everyone was amazed, and experts ranked him among the top quarterbacks.

Representatives from 28 NFL teams gathered at Texas Tech to see Patrick in action during his pro day. He became one of the fastest-rising stars during the draft process, having an impressive 18 private workouts and team visits — the most for any player in 2017. Coaches from teams like the Arizona Cardinals, New Orleans Saints, Cincinnati Bengals, Los Angeles Chargers, Cleveland Browns, Chicago Bears, and Pittsburgh Steelers were eager to see his incredible skills.

Finally, the big day arrived. The Kansas City Chiefs, a professional NFL team, chose Patrick Mahomes in the first round of the 2017 NFL Draft, making him the 10th overall pick. It was a momentous occasion for Patrick and for the Chiefs, who hadn't picked a quarterback in the first round since way back in 1983.

The Chiefs were so excited to have Patrick on their team that they traded up to get him, exchanging their first-round pick, a third-round pick, and their first-round pick for the next year. Patrick signed a fantastic four-year, $16.42 million contract, guaranteeing his place in the NFL and making his dreams a reality.

As the 2017 season unfolded, Patrick's moment to shine came sooner than expected. With the Chiefs already securing a playoff spot, they decided to rest their starting quarterback and give Patrick his first career start. The game against the Broncos was a thrilling one, and Patrick showcased his skills brilliantly. Completing 22 of 35 passes for 284 yards, he helped lead the Chiefs to a 27–24 win, marking the beginning of an extraordinary journey in the NFL for Patrick Mahomes.

CHAPTER 5

Becoming a Superstar

In January 2018, the Chiefs made a special announcement: Patrick was going to be the starting quarterback! In his very first game as the starting quarterback, the Chiefs faced off against their rivals, the Chargers. Patrick threw for 256 yards and an amazing four touchdowns, leading the Chiefs to victory with a score of 38–28. His incredible performance earned him the title of AFC Offensive Player of the Week.

The following week was even more spectacular. Patrick threw for a whopping 326 yards and six touchdowns in a single game! He set the record for the most touchdown passes in a quarterback's first three career games and the most touchdown passes in the first two weeks of a season. He won the AFC Offensive Player of the Week award again, a rare feat for any quarterback.

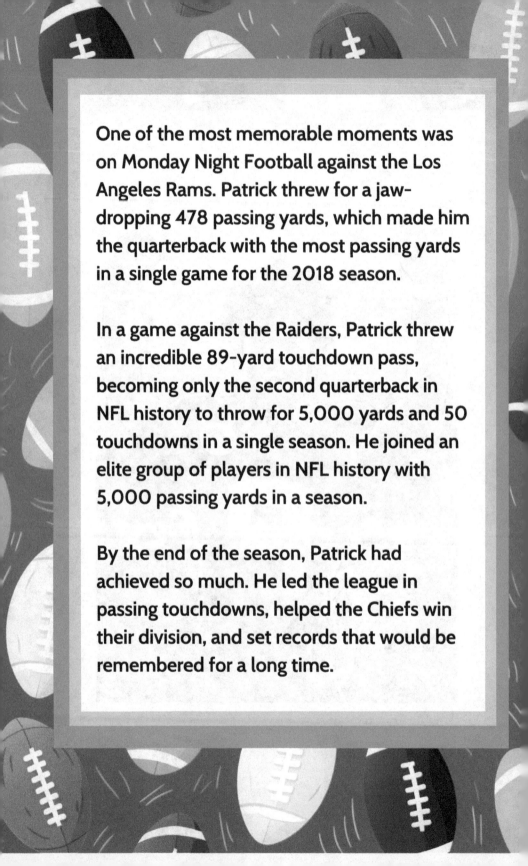

One of the most memorable moments was on Monday Night Football against the Los Angeles Rams. Patrick threw for a jaw-dropping 478 passing yards, which made him the quarterback with the most passing yards in a single game for the 2018 season.

In a game against the Raiders, Patrick threw an incredible 89-yard touchdown pass, becoming only the second quarterback in NFL history to throw for 5,000 yards and 50 touchdowns in a single season. He joined an elite group of players in NFL history with 5,000 passing yards in a season.

By the end of the season, Patrick had achieved so much. He led the league in passing touchdowns, helped the Chiefs win their division, and set records that would be remembered for a long time.

The Chiefs didn't just stop at the regular season; they made it to the playoffs. In the Divisional Round, they defeated the Indianapolis Colts, giving the Chiefs their first home playoff win in a long, long time. Patrick played an amazing game, throwing for 278 yards and rushing for a touchdown.

Although the Chiefs lost a tough game to the Patriots in the AFC Championship, Patrick's performance throughout the season was extraordinary.

For his outstanding season, Patrick received numerous awards. He was chosen for the Pro Bowl, named First Team All–Pro, and even won the prestigious NFL MVP award, making history for the Chiefs franchise. His fellow players ranked him as the fourth-best player on the NFL Top 100 Players of 2019.

CHAPTER 6

Super Bowl Glory

In the 2019 season, Patrick Mahomes continued his incredible journey, turning every game into a thrilling story filled with triumphs and unforgettable moments.

In the first game against the Jacksonville Jaguars, Patrick faced a challenge when star receiver Tyreek Hill got injured in the first quarter. But Patrick, with his magical arm, threw for 378 yards and three touchdowns. Even with a little ankle sprain in the second quarter, he showed everyone that challenges couldn't stop him.

In the next game against the Raiders, Patrick put on a dazzling performance. In just the second quarter, he threw for 278 yards and four touchdowns, the most passing yards in any quarter since 2008! His amazing game earned him the title of AFC Offensive Player of the Week.

For the second year in a row, Patrick was named AFC Offensive Player of the Month for September. Imagine leading the Chiefs to a perfect 4–0 start with 10 passing touchdowns and no interceptions – Patrick was truly a football wizard!

In week 7 against the Denver Broncos, Patrick faced a tough moment when he dislocated his patella. But the next day, everyone breathed a sigh of relief when the MRI revealed no serious damage. Patrick, like a true hero, returned just two weeks later against the Tennessee Titans.

Throughout the season, Patrick showed his versatility. In a victory over the Chargers, he ran for a career-high 59 yards, celebrating with a special gesture that reminded everyone he was the 10th overall pick in the 2017 NFL Draft. He finished the season with 4,031 yards, 26 touchdowns, and only five interceptions.

As the playoffs arrived, Patrick's magic reached new heights. In the Divisional Round against the Houston Texans, the Chiefs faced a daunting 24–0 deficit. But Patrick led a spectacular comeback, throwing for 321 yards and five touchdowns and rushing for 53 yards. The Chiefs won an incredible 51–31 victory, showcasing their resilience.

In the AFC Championship against the Titans, Patrick continued his heroics. He threw for three touchdowns, rushed for a 27-yard touchdown – the second longest run of his career – and sparked a comeback to a 35–24 victory. The Chiefs were on their way to the Super Bowl for the first time in 50 years!

Super Bowl LIV brought another epic moment. The Chiefs trailed 20–10 against the San Francisco 49ers in the fourth quarter. With less than 8 minutes remaining, Patrick called for a special play called Jet Chip Wasp. In a magical play, he completed a deep pass to Tyreek Hill, changing the course of the game. The Chiefs went on a 21–0 run, securing their first Super Bowl victory in five decades.

For his outstanding performance, Patrick was named Super Bowl MVP—the youngest quarterback and third-youngest player in NFL history to earn this incredible award. His fellow players ranked him fourth on the NFL Top 100 Players of 2020, solidifying his status as a football legend. The 2019 season was a fairy tale of triumph, courage, and Super Bowl glory for Patrick Mahomes!

CHAPTER 7

Second Super Bowl Victory

In the thrilling 2022 season, Patrick Mahomes continued his extraordinary journey, creating magic on the football field. In Week 1, he threw for a sensational 360 yards and five touchdowns, securing a resounding victory against the Cardinals. This stellar performance earned him the AFC Offensive Player of the Week title.

Throughout the season, Mahomes broke records and achieved remarkable milestones. Notably, he set single-game franchise records for pass completions and attempts, breaking NFL records for passing yards in a quarterback's first 75 starts. His excellence was recognized with the AFC Offensive Player of the Month award for November.

Despite a high ankle sprain in the Divisional Round, Mahomes returned to guide the Chiefs to victory, setting the stage for an impressive AFC Championship win against the Bengals. In Super Bowl LVII against the Eagles, he faced adversity with an ankle re-aggravation but led a stunning comeback, securing a 38–35 win. Mahomes was awarded his second career Super Bowl MVP.

The 2022 season concluded with Mahomes as the league leader in both passing yards and touchdowns, earning him the Most Valuable Player title. He achieved a historic feat, becoming the first player in NFL history to accomplish all four major feats in a single season.

In September 2023, Mahomes and the Chiefs made history by restructuring his contract, making him the highest-paid player in NFL history over a four-season span. The 2023 season unfolded with more milestones, including Mahomes reaching his 200th career touchdown and becoming the youngest quarterback to defeat all other 31 teams besides his own.

Despite facing challenges and his receivers leading the league in dropped passes, Mahomes showcased resilience. He overcame a 14-point deficit against the Las Vegas Raiders, earning another AFC Offensive Player of the Week honor.

With victories over the Miami Dolphins and the Buffalo Bills, Mahomes propelled the Chiefs to their sixth consecutive AFC Championship Game, marking the second-longest streak in history. In the game against the Bills, Mahomes, along with tight end Travis Kelce, broke the record for most career touchdowns in the playoffs for a quarterback/receiver duo.

Patrick Mahomes' 2022 and 2023 seasons showcased his skill, resilience, and ability to lead his team to victory on the grandest stage. The legend of Mahomes continued to grow as he etched his name in NFL history once again.

CHAPTER 8

Off the field

On a special day, September 1, 2020, Patrick Mahomes asked his high school sweetheart, Brittany Matthews, to be his forever partner. It happened in a cozy suite in Arrowhead Stadium, where Mahomes had just received his Super Bowl LIV championship ring. Brittany, not just a soccer player but also a certified personal trainer, became a co-owner of the Kansas City Current, a professional women's soccer team.

The lovebirds married on March 12, 2022, and now, they're a happy family with a daughter and a son.

You might catch Patrick Mahomes on your screen in the NFL Films and Netflix series called Quarterback. This show, featuring Mahomes, along with quarterbacks Kirk Cousins and Marcus Mariota, gives us a glimpse of their lives on and off the field during the 2022 season. The series premiered on Netflix on July 12, 2023, with Mahomes himself involved in its production through his newly-founded 2PM Productions.

In April 2019, he shared some incredible news – the launch of a nonprofit called the *"15 and the Mahomies Foundation"*. This special organization is all about making kids' lives better.

Patrick believed that with great success came an even greater responsibility to give back. He encouraged others, young and old, to join hands in creating a world where everyone had an equal chance to succeed. Through his foundation and various initiatives, he showcased that kindness and generosity had the power to transform lives.

But Patrick doesn't stop there. He and his teammate Tyrann Mathieu encouraged people to vote in the 2020 Presidential Election through a special project in Kansas City. They even teamed up with basketball star LeBron James and his Rock the Vote initiative to spread the word. Patrick Mahomes' actions and dedication to making positive change earned him a spot on Time 100's list of most influential people in both 2020 and 2023. He's like a real-life hero making a difference!

CHAPTER 9

Inspirational Lessons

Patrick's life and career taught us that no dream is too big. Whether you dream of being a sports star, a scientist, or an artist, you can reach for the stars. Patrick started as a kid with a passion for football, just like you might have a passion for something special.

Hard work and dedication were Patrick's best teammates. He didn't become a football wizard overnight; he practiced, he stumbled, and he tried again. Each day was a chance to get better, and that's a lesson we can all carry with us.

Imagine Patrick tossing footballs under the bright Texas sky, practicing again and again. It wasn't always easy, but he never gave up. That's the secret sauce—hard work! Just like learning a new game or a tricky subject, it takes effort, but each step gets you closer to your goal.

Patrick didn't just play football; he lived it. Dedication means sticking with something even when it gets tough. Just like Patrick faced challenges, you might face tough times too. But remember, dedication turns challenges into victories.

Patrick's story is like a guidebook, showing us that dreams are meant to be chased. Whatever you love, go for it with all your might. Whether you dream of scoring goals, painting masterpieces, or exploring outer space, the world is waiting for your unique talents.

Remember the lessons you learned from Patrick's journey. Believe in your dreams, work hard, and never forget the power of dedication. You're like a shooting star with endless possibilities. So, as you read these pages and close this book, know that you hold the pen to your own inspiring story.

Your journey starts now. Dream big, work hard, and let your journey be as magical as Patrick's. The world is ready for the wonderful tale that only you can write!

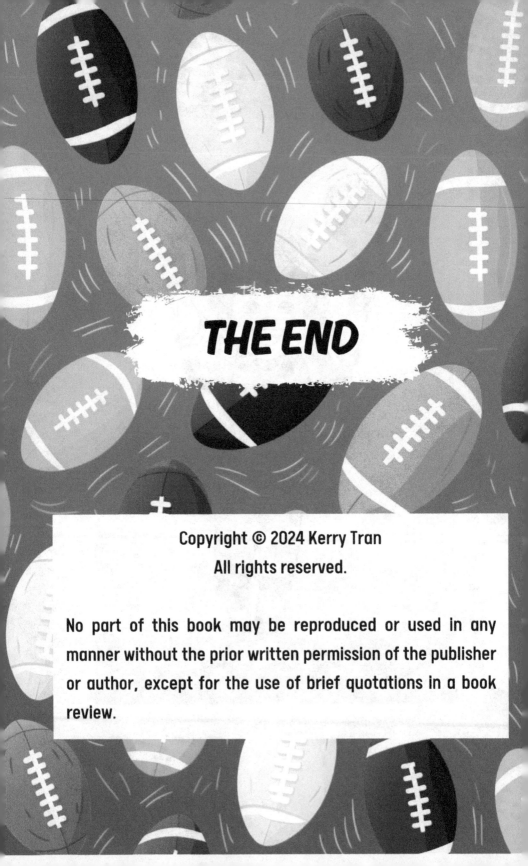

THE END

Made in the USA
Monee, IL
22 October 2024

68449750R00046